Straight Talk About...
# TEEN
# PREGNANCY

Pamela
McDowell

Crabtree Publishing Company
www.crabtreebooks.com

Straight Talk About...

**Developed and produced by:** Plan B Book Packagers

**Editorial director:** Ellen Rodger

**Art director:** Rosie Gowsell-Pattison

**Fictional Introductions:** Rachel Eagen

**Editor:** Molly Aloian

**Project coordinator:** Kathy Middleton

**Production coordinator:** Margaret Amy Salter

**Prepress technician:** Margaret Amy Salter

**Consultant:** Susan Rodger, PhD., C. Psych., Psychologist and Professor Faculty of Education, The University of Western Ontario

**Photographs:**
Title page: f00sion/iStockPhoto.com; p. 4: Piotr Marcinski/Shutterstock Inc.; p. 6: quavondo/ iStockPhoto.com; p. 8: (top) ducu59us/Shutterstock Inc., (bottom) Monkey Business Images/Shutterstock Inc.; p. 9: iStockPhoto.com; p. 10: Justin Paget/Shutterstock Inc.; p. 11: Simone van den Berg/Shutterstock Inc.; p. 12: Karina Bakalyan/Shutterstock Inc.; p. 13: iStockPhoto.com; p. 14: Mandy Godbehear/Shutterstock Inc.; p. 16: Lev Olkha/Shutterstock Inc.; p. 17: Junial Enterprises/Shutterstock Inc.; p. 18: (bottom) Mikael Damkier/Shutterstock Inc., (top) jscreations/ Shutterstock Inc.; p. 19: Marcin-linfernum/Shutterstock Inc.; p. 20: mick20/Shutterstock Inc.; p. 22: Dmitriy Shironosov/Shutterstock Inc.; p. 23: Sergey Furtaev/ Shutterstock Inc.; p. 24: Lightpoet/Shutterstock Inc.; p. 26: Shape Charge/iStockPhoto.com; p. 28: Zsolt Nyulaszi/Shutterstock Inc.; p. 30: sdominick/ iStockPhoto.com; p. 32: Bogdan Ionescu/Shutterstock Inc.; p. 33: Rob Marmion/Shutterstock Inc.; p. 34: cjp/ iStockPhoto.com; p. 36: Aldo Murillo/iStockPhoto.com; p. 37: Poulsons Photography/Shutterstock Inc.; p. 38: Justin Paget/Shutterstock Inc.; p. 39: J. Tyler/ iStockPhoto.com; p. 40: iStockPhoto.com

**Library and Archives Canada Cataloguing in Publication**

McDowell, Pamela
   Teen pregnancy / Pamela McDowell.

(Straight talk about--)
Includes index.
Issued also in an electronic format.
ISBN 978-0-7787-2132-1 (bound).--ISBN 978-0-7787-2139-0 (pbk.)

   1. Teenage mothers--Juvenile literature. 2. Teenage pregnancy--Juvenile literature. 3. Youth--Sexual behavior--Juvenile literature. I. Title. II. Series: Straight talk about-- (St. Catharines, Ont.)

HQ759.4.M355 2010     j306.874'3     C2010-902769-8

**Library of Congress Cataloging-in-Publication Data**

McDowell, Pamela.
   Teen pregnancy / Pamela McDowell.
     p. cm. -- (Straight talk about--)
   Includes index.
   ISBN 978-0-7787-2139-0 (pbk. : alk. paper) --
ISBN 978-0-7787-2132-1 (reinforced library binding : alk. paper)
-- ISBN 978-1-4271-9545-6 (electronic (pdf))
   1. Teenage mothers--Juvenile literature. 2. Teenage pregnancy--Juvenile literature. 3. Youth--Sexual behavior--Juvenile literature. I. Title. II. Series.

HQ759.4.M333 2010
306.874'3--dc22
                                2010016409

## Crabtree Publishing Company

www.crabtreebooks.com     1-800-387-7650

Printed in China/082010/AP20100512

**Published in Canada**
**Crabtree Publishing**
616 Welland Ave.
St. Catharines, ON
L2M 5V6

**Published in the United States**
**Crabtree Publishing**
PMB 59051
350 Fifth Avenue, 59th Floor
New York, NY 10118

**Published in the United Kingdom**
**Crabtree Publishing**
Maritime House
Basin Road North, Hove
BN41 1WR

**Published in Australia**
**Crabtree Publishing**
386 Mt. Alexander Rd.
Ascot Vale (Melbourne)
VIC 3032

# CONTENTS

Sam knocked on the bathroom door.

"Come on, I have to go!"

The door creaked open. Tina glared at him. Her eyes were red and swollen. She'd been crying. Mom appeared behind Tina, looking really serious. The crease between her eyebrows was deep and worried.

"I, uh...I have to go." He pushed past them and shut the door. Downstairs, he heard hushed voices talking very quickly. He heard his sister start to cry again.

He finished up and walked down to the kitchen. Mom and Tina were sitting at the table. Mom was stirring a cup of tea, still with that worried expression on her face.

"Come and sit down, Sam."

He sat across from his sister. She started to sob into the sleeve of her sweater. She wouldn't look at him.

"Honey, Tina has some sad news. We were going to wait to tell you until Dad knew, but you might as well know now."

"Tina, what's wrong?" Sam had never seen his sister cry like this.

"Sam, your sister's pregnant."

Pregnant? Tina was only 16. How could she be pregnant?

"We're going to have to make some changes around here." Mom sipped her tea and looked at Tina carefully, then placed her hand on Tina's. "It's going to be a bit rough but we'll get through it."

# Introduction
# A World Changer

Each year, many teenagers get pregnant and often the pregnancy is not planned. It can be really hard on them and their families. The decisions they have to make, whether to have the baby or not, keep it or put the baby up for adoption, are important and difficult.

Each choice brings change. Some teens opt to keep their babies. The challenge of raising a child brings a lot of stress into the lives of teenagers. For many, new responsibilities make it very hard to go to school or live life the way they did before.

In this book, you will learn about teen pregnancy, your options, and where you can go to get support if you or someone you care about becomes pregnant.

"I don't regret having my baby but I kind of wish I had more time to myself. She cries a lot and I don't understand it. It makes me so frustrated when she cries and I can't do anything about it."
Marisol, aged 16.

# Chapter 1
# Teen Pregnancy

Over 750,000 teen girls get pregnant each year in the United States. That's more than in any other **developed** country. This number is three times the teen pregnancy rate in Canada and seven times higher than Denmark and Sweden!

Three out of ten girls will get pregnant at least once before they are 20 years old. Your body may be ready to have a baby when you are 13 or 16 years old, but it is hard to prepare yourself for pregnancy and babies when in many ways, you are still growing up yourself.

Pregnancy can be emotionally and physically trying at any age. **Hormones** affect how your body feels and how you feel emotionally. Pregnancy can make you feel joy, sadness, excitement, and fear all at the same time. There are so many decisions to make and so many tough choices. How do you know when you have made the right one for you?

# How Does It Happen?

Teenagers have sex for a lot of reasons.
They might want do it because their friends
are doing it. They might have sex to be close
to someone special. They may be curious, or
they might be doing it against their will. The reasons
a young person is having sex can sometimes make a
difference in what they do to prevent pregnancy and **sexually
transmitted infections** (STIs). Sometimes teens ignore birth
control. Some teens do not have access to birth control or
cannot afford it. Sometimes, the male partner will refuse to
use birth control and insist that "it's alright." Other teen
pregnancies happen when birth control fails or when teens are
under the influence of drugs or alcohol.

Alcohol and drugs lower **inhibitions**, which means you are more
likely to do things you would normally think twice about doing.

## Forced Sex and Rape

Some teen pregnancies are the result of forced sex or sexual assault. Nearly 20 percent of teen pregnancies are caused by unwanted sexual activity or rape. Rape is a crime. Often, teens who have been raped or **coerced** into sex feel fearful or shocked. These feelings may worsen if they discover they are pregnant. It is important to remember that help is available for any physical and emotional injuries. If reported to a doctor or hospital early enough, pregnancy can be prevented.

## Planned Pregnancies

Sometimes getting pregnant and having a baby is a **conscious** choice. Teens who intend to get pregnant do so for many reasons. Some have older boyfriends who want them to get pregnant. Others have unstable homes or no clear idea of future goals or careers. Having babies early is also sometimes a cultural or family choice for teens who have young parents themselves.

Sometimes, when a friend or sibling has had a child at a young age, other teens feel less afraid to have children.

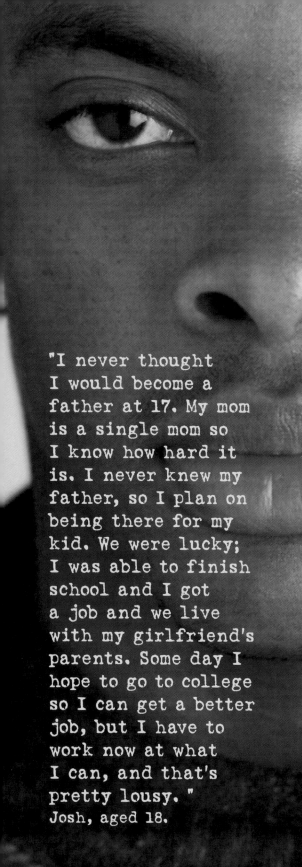

"I never thought I would become a father at 17. My mom is a single mom so I know how hard it is. I never knew my father, so I plan on being there for my kid. We were lucky; I was able to finish school and I got a job and we live with my girlfriend's parents. Some day I hope to go to college so I can get a better job, but I have to work now at what I can, and that's pretty lousy. "
Josh, aged 18.

## Risky Business

There are a lot of things to think about when you get involved in a relationship and are thinking about having sex. You risk getting pregnant every time you have sex. Most teenagers are uncomfortable thinking about their sexuality. Some think that learning about your body and how it works is creepy. This makes planning ahead difficult because it means admitting that you want to have sex.

## Waiting and Planning

You have many options when it comes to sex, but if you don't have a plan, there are a lot of things that can influence a decision you might regret. Choosing to wait to have sex is a good way to protect your feelings, your health, and your future. If you choose not to wait, using safe and effective methods of birth control can safeguard your future.

# What Are the Signs of Pregnancy?

Your body changes a lot during **puberty** and throughout your teens. It can be hard to get used to the new you. If you don't understand how your body works, it can be hard to recognize if you are pregnant.

The early signs of pregnancy can be just like how your body feels before your period. You might feel moody and tired, your breasts may be tender, and you may need to pee often. You may develop dizziness, a dull backache, and a slight fever. You might miss your period or it might be very light. Drugstore pregnancy tests can confirm if you are pregnant, but sometimes they give false negatives, especially early on in a pregnancy. It is important to confirm your suspicions with a pregnancy test from your doctor or a clinic. Ignoring the signs could put your health in danger.

Home pregnancy tests can confirm you are pregnant, but you still need to go to a doctor to look after your health.

# A Life Changer

Pregnant teens are changed by the serious decisions they have to make. Most pregnant teen mothers, particularly those who choose to keep their babies, drop out of school. Many only temporarily have the support of their baby's father, if at all. Some lose the support of their parents. If they keep their babies, statistics show that most teen moms live in **poverty** as a single parent and their children are more likely to not finish school, get pregnant early themselves, or spend time in jail. Statistics also show that almost a quarter of teen mothers have another baby within two years of the first. People don't set out to become statistics. Many teen parents intend to get married and continue their education, but the hard realities of parenthood often split them apart and end their education.

Pregnancy is often the easy part of parenthood. Most teen parents who opt to keep their babies never finish high school and always struggle to make ends meet.

## Decisions, Decisions

Pregnancy forces teen mothers and fathers to make decisions that have lifelong **consequences**. How do I tell the people I love that I am pregnant or that my girlfriend is pregnant? Do I end the pregnancy or have the baby? Should I keep the baby or give it up for adoption? What will people think of my choices? What will they think of me? There may be so many people who could be disappointed or upset about decisions a pregnant teen makes, including parents, siblings, and friends. The most important thing to remember is that if you are pregnant, the choice of what to do about it is ultimately yours, and so is the responsibility.

## Truth and Consequences

The risks and consequences of teen pregnancy are clear. So why are so many teenage girls getting pregnant? It is much easier to prevent a pregnancy than it is to **terminate** one or to have a baby while very young. **Abstinence** is often difficult to maintain for many teens. For others, birth control is a touchy subject. You might worry that it looks like you are expecting sex if you carry a condom or take birth control pills. You might fear your parents' reaction if they found out. It is hard to be strong and in charge of your own body when so many conflicting feelings get in the way.

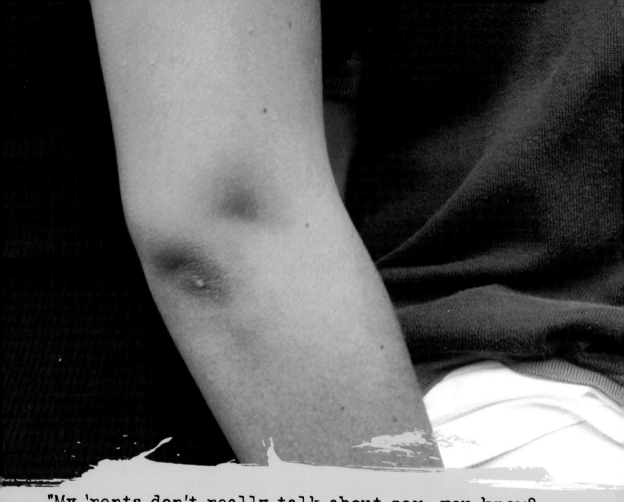

"My 'rents don't really talk about sex, you know?
Except to say that I better not be getting into
trouble. I mean, I haven't had sex and they act
like the sex police. They don't know anything
about my life but they think they do."
-Charlene, aged 15.

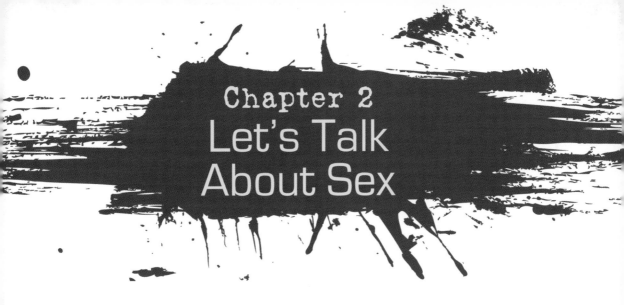

# Chapter 2
# Let's Talk About Sex

Okay, let's back up a bit. Sex is a natural part of life—it's how we all got here, right? But how, exactly, does it all work?

## Puberty Changes Everything

Technically speaking, puberty is the time when your body produces hormones that prepare you for sexual maturity. Sexual maturity means being capable of reproducing, or having babies. It may seem like you go from a child's body to a young adult's body almost overnight. You may grow quickly and feel clumsy and awkward. You may also notice hair in places you didn't have any before, like on your legs, in your armpits, and around your genitals.

Puberty can be confusing, scary, and exciting all at the same time. You may feel a lot more emotional than usual. You might feel butterflies in the pit of your stomach when you see a certain boy or girl in the hallway at school. Or you might find yourself thinking about sex all the time. You can thank your hormones for that.

# Girl Changes

For girls, hormones cause your hips and breasts to change and grow. Once your body changes, you might notice that other people, especially boys your own age and even older men, treat you differently. It is natural for you to have mixed feelings about the extra attention that can come with puberty. You might feel happy and excited about the new ways people notice you, but it can make you feel uncomfortable and nervous, too. Feeling comfortable about your body and the changes that are happening will help others to understand that you are confident and strong.

# Getting Your Period

Around age 11 to 16 (it's different for everyone), you may begin menstruating, or getting your period. The menstrual cycle is your body's way of preparing itself for a possible pregnancy. Your ovaries will release an egg each month which will travel down the **fallopian tubes** toward the **uterus**. This is called ovulation. Throughout the month, the lining of your uterus will thicken with blood and cells in preparation for a pregnancy. If the egg is fertilized with **sperm**, you will become pregnant and the fertilized egg will attach itself to your uterus where a fetus will develop. If no fertilized egg arrives in the uterus, this lining is shed through the vagina during menstruation. Menstruation lasts three to seven days each month. During your lifetime, you will ovulate or release only about 400 of the 400,000 eggs you were born with. With the release of that very first egg, it is now possible for you to become pregnant.

## Boy Changes

For boys, the changes during puberty are just as dramatic. People may also treat you differently and have different expectations for your behavior as you become a young adult. This might not always feel comfortable or right.

## Squeaky Voice and Facial Hair

During puberty, your shoulders will grow broader and your voice may slip and squeak before it gets deeper. You will begin to grow hair on your face and body. Your testes (testicles) will begin to produce sperm, and you may notice that your penis gets hard from time to time. This is called an erection.

Wet dreams are one way your body tests out its new sexual maturity. Ejaculating in your sleep during a wet dream is normal and uncontrollable. When this happens, sperm and other fluids are discharged from the penis as semen. Your body is now ready for reproduction, even if you aren't.

Hormone changes during puberty can cause skin problems, such as acne, as well as increased sweating.

## Conception Story

To make a baby, a sperm must fertilize an egg. During sexual intercourse, the erect penis ejaculates in the vagina, sending millions of sperm swimming in search of an egg. When one sperm succeeds in fertilizing the egg, conception has occurred and pregnancy begins.

The new **embryo** combines **genetic** information from the mother and father to create a unique individual. Within a few days to a week, the embryo implants itself in the uterus, or womb, where it will continue to grow for the next 40 weeks. The **placenta** forms the bond between the developing embryo and the uterus, providing **nutrients** and oxygen.

## Birth Story

At eight weeks, the embryo is nearly an inch long and is called a fetus. The organs, fingers, and skeleton begin to develop during the next month, and by the end of the fourth month, the fetus will be six inches (15 cm) long. At 20 weeks, the fetus can open and close its eyes and suck its thumb. During the last ten weeks of pregnancy, the fetus will be very active and will grow quickly. When it is time for labor to begin, contractions of the powerful muscles of the uterus will push the baby out through the mother's vagina.

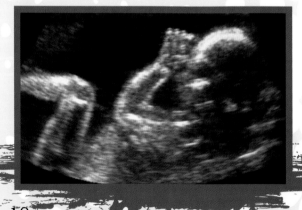

# Preventing Pregnancy

There are a lot of myths and strange stories that surround pregnancy prevention and birth control. You've probably heard some of them, such as if you have have sex standing up or during your period, you won't get pregnant. You might have learned from a friend that having a bath right after sex or pushing hard on your belly button afterward will prevent pregnancy. These stories are silly. They are about as effective at preventing pregnancy as wishing and hoping.

Babies are cute, but they also cry a lot and require a lot of attention.

Of course, the only surefire way to prevent pregnancy is to abstain, or not have sex, but many methods of birth control are very effective at preventing pregnancy, if used regularly and properly.

# Consistency Matters

If birth control is not used the first time and every single time you have sex, the risk of pregnancy grows. A sexually active teenage girl who does not use contraceptives has a 90 percent chance of getting pregnant within a year. Withdrawal, or removing the penis just before ejaculation, is not an effective method of birth control. A small amount of fluid leaks from the penis prior to ejaculation and can cause pregnancy.

# Condoms, Pills, and Other Methods

Condoms are the contraceptive most easily available to teens. Also known as safes or rubbers, condoms are sold at pharmacies and other stores without a prescription. A **latex** condom that is used properly over the erect penis prior to contact with the vagina, will prevent pregnancy 97 percent of the time.

The birth control pill, commonly known as "the pill," has been around for decades. It must be prescribed to a teenage girl by a doctor. The pill acts by changing hormone levels to prevent the release of an egg during ovulation. The pill is 95 to 98 percent effective, if taken consistently, the same time each day. The birth control patch and shot are newer hormonal contraceptives which must also be given by a doctor. Several other methods of birth control must also be prescribed by a doctor.

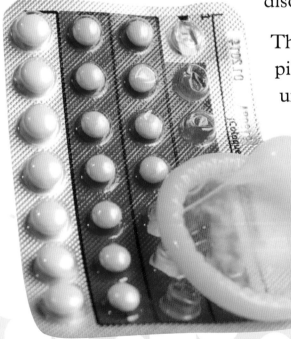

The emergency contraception pill prevents pregnancy after unplanned, unprotected sex has occurred. The ECP can be obtained from a clinic or pharmacy and must be taken within 72 hours. It is not an abortion pill, but is 89 percent effective in preventing pregnancy before it begins.

# Pregnancy Prevention Myths

People have been trying to prevent pregnancy for thousands of years. In ancient times, women jumped up and down after sex to try to prevent sperm from swimming upwards. They also drank tea made with poisonous herbs. Today, reliable and effective birth control is available from stores and pharmacies, but still myths prevail about magical contraceptives. Don't trust the rumors. Here are some common sex, disease prevention, and contraception myths:

**I won't get pregnant the first time I have sex.**

This simply isn't true. You can get pregnant the first time or any time you have unprotected sex.

**I won't catch any diseases. My partner is very clean.**

You can't tell if your partner has a disease by looking at them. A sexually transmitted infection (STI) such as HIV, herpes, and human papillomavirus (HPV) are transmitted through unprotected sexual intercourse, oral, and anal sex. Condoms are the only birth control method that limits exposure to STIs.

**I heard that using two condoms can double my protection.**

Using two condoms at the same time will cause friction and may actually increase the risk that one or both condoms will break. Unopened condoms should not be stored in a warm place, like a wallet, because the latex can begin to deteriorate. A condom should also never be used more than once.

"My best friend and I took a **virginity pledge** and got abstinence rings. She didn't stick by her pledge the next year and actually said she didn't even make one. She totally lied about it. I'm still sticking with mine. It means something to me."
Bethany, aged 17.

# Chapter 3
# Relationships

Relationships can be confusing, especially when you are new to them. Becoming intimate with a boyfriend or girlfriend can be both exciting and scary. You might wonder if you love this person or if they love you. Expressing your feelings can be difficult. How do you tell someone what you want in a relationship? What if they don't want the same things? What if they reject you for not doing what they want?

Many teens feel they must have sex, even if they are not ready, in order to show or prove their love to a boyfriend or girlfriend. Loving relationships are supposed to be relationships of equality, where partners are independent individuals who support and understand each other. They are not controlling or **conditional**. If a person loves you, they won't make fun of you for speaking your mind. They shouldn't reject you if you decide you are not ready to have sex or if you want to use protection to prevent pregnancy.

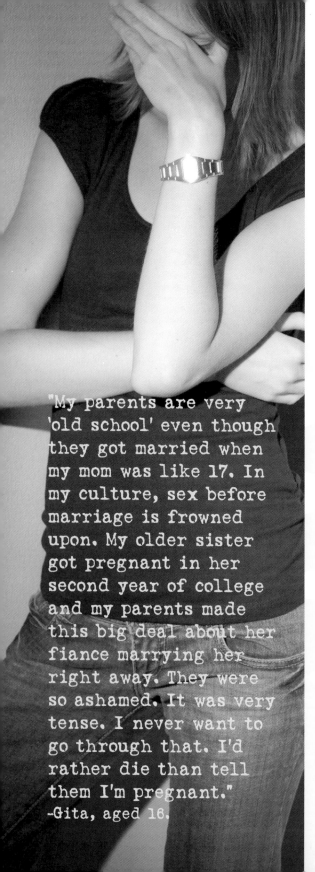

"My parents are very 'old school' even though they got married when my mom was like 17. In my culture, sex before marriage is frowned upon. My older sister got pregnant in her second year of college and my parents made this big deal about her fiance marrying her right away. They were so ashamed. It was very tense. I never want to go through that. I'd rather die than tell them I'm pregnant."
-Gita, aged 16.

## Model Relationships

We learn a lot about relationships from the people around us—our family and friends. Often, our **ethical**, and religious beliefs are passed down from our parents. Sometimes, parents have beliefs that differ from those in the dominant society. For example, they may believe that sex before marriage is wrong, or that women should have children young and not put effort into schooling or preparing for a future that delays motherhood. New relationships sometimes challenge these beliefs.

Teens may act without much thought so they don't have to feel like they are disappointing others. This is often described as "getting carried away." Having sex is a big deal. It's important to know your own mind and prepare and protect yourself emotionally and physically.

# Under Pressure

Peer pressure can be a good motivator to study and get good marks or join a club or team, but it can also cause us to do things our gut tells us are wrong. Resisting the pressure to do drugs or alcohol, or have sex before you are ready can be tough if you are convinced everybody's doing it. Rest assured, they aren't. Only 20 percent of 15 year olds and 48 percent of high school students have had sexual intercourse, and in studies, most of them say they wish they had waited.

# At Risk

Sometimes it is difficult to wait because a boyfriend or girlfriend is pressuring you to have sex. Teen girls in relationships with older boys or men are more likely to become pregnant. Some studies show that two-thirds of the babies born to teen mothers are fathered by men older than high school age.

Each state has laws that set out the age of consent, or the age when the law says you can agree to have sex. In Canada, it is the same age across the country. Men who are older than the age of consent and who have sex with teens younger than the age can be charged with **statutory rape**. Older men are more likely to force sex and are less likely to wear condoms. Teens involved in violent relationships are also more likely to get pregnant. Dating violence is an act of power, not of love. Manipulating someone into having sex or coercing them into having sex without protection is abuse.

"I was terrified. I didn't know what to do or who to
tell. I felt like I let everyone down because they
were expecting more from me. I did well, was a good
girl, and now this."
Casey aged 16.

# Chapter 4
## Staying Healthy

Getting pregnant may not be something you worry about much—until the moment you think you are. Suddenly it's always on your mind, along with the next question: What do I do now?

You may get all kinds of advice from friends. It is hard to know what to believe. If you don't have anyone whose advice you can trust, a clinic can help in these first anxious moments. Some clinics and health centers offer free pregnancy tests, counseling services, and information about pregnancy and the decisions you need to make.

## Seek Medical Attention

See a doctor as soon as possible to begin **prenatal** care. A doctor can give you a pregnancy test and estimate your baby's due date. An internal pelvic exam, blood test, urine test, and sexually transmitted infection (STI) tests will help to assess your overall health. Denying the pregnancy won't make it go away and could put you and the baby at risk. No matter what you decide to do about the pregnancy, you need to stay healthy.

## Prenatal Care

Teens are at a greater risk of **anemia** and high blood pressure during pregnancy. Babies born to teen moms are sometimes early and underweight. A doctor can advise you on nutrition and vitamins needed for a healthy pregnancy. You should continue to see a doctor throughout your pregnancy. This may require visits once a month for the first 28 weeks, then more frequently until the birth of the baby.

## What Happens There?

During your doctor or clinic appointments, your weight, blood pressure, and urine will be checked. The doctor will measure your abdomen and listen to the baby's heartbeat. An **ultrasound** may be done to make sure the baby is developing well. If you experience bleeding or pain, you should see your doctor immediately, even if you are not planning to continue the pregnancy. You and your baby could be at risk. Twelve percent of teen pregnancies end with a miscarriage for many different reasons. After a miscarriage, you may feel sadness, guilt, or relief. It is important to talk about your feelings with a trusted adult or parent.

An ultrasound can pinpoint your baby's due date.

# Pregnancy Self-care

When you first discover you are pregnant, you may be overwhelmed. You may feel fear, guilt, shame, anger, sadness, and excitement—or all of these things combined. This can be a stressful time. You need to take care of yourself both physically and emotionally. Here are some things to do:

Now is the time to turn to others for support. This could be the baby's father, your family and friends, or a professional, such as a doctor, counselor, or teacher. Get advice on whether you can finish school. More than half of teen mothers do not graduate from high school, which severely limits their futures.

Drugs are harmful to you and your baby but it might not be easy to stop. If you smoke cigarettes or do drugs, let a health care professional know. They can help you kick your habits without doing more harm.

Stop drinking alcohol. Alcohol is also passed directly to the unborn baby where it affects brain development and can cause fetal alcohol spectrum disorder (FASD), which is a birth defect. Even a few drinks is enough to do permanent damage.

Everything you put in your body affects your unborn baby. Aspirin and cough medicine can harm your baby, too. A doctor or pharmacist can give you advice on the risks before you take these.

Your baby will take nutrients from your body to grow. Dieting or not eating well could put your health in danger. Pregnant women are more susceptible to cold or flu viruses as their immune systems are working harder.

"With my second pregnancy, I was older and more settled. I chose to keep the baby. I had an abortion many years earlier, and although I don't regret it, I did think a lot about how I chose to keep one baby and not the other."
Callie, aged 23.

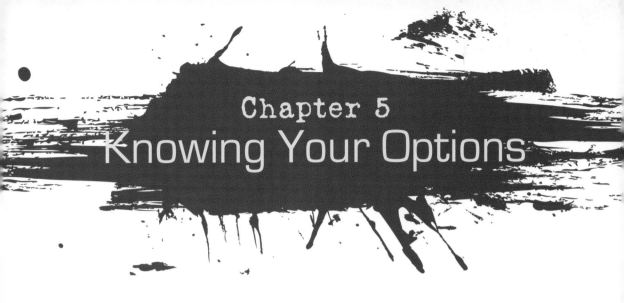

# Chapter 5
# Knowing Your Options

Once you have confirmed that you are pregnant and healthy, you need to make some decisions. Your family, culture, religious beliefs, values, and personal hopes and dreams will all influence your decisions, but only you can make them—it is your body and your life. Take the time to gather information. Know and understand your feelings. There are no right or wrong decisions, but some options may be better for you at this time in your life.

## Keeping the Baby

Many teens choose to keep their babies. This means they raise them on their own, or with the support of their parents or parent, or the baby's father. For a teen still in school, raising a child on their own often means using welfare or social assistance, which does not provide much to live on. Even if a teen mother or father has a job, chances are it is low paying and does not provide drug or health benefits. The overwhelming majority of teen parents and their children live in poverty.

31

"If I ever get to meet my son's biological parents, I would give them the biggest hug! I want them to know how deeply grateful we are to them for making what must have been a very painful and difficult decision."
Stella, adoptive parent.

# Raising a Baby

Putting someone else's needs first every hour of every day is a huge sacrifice. The bond between a mother and baby can be a wonderful thing, but parenting demands more than love. It is difficult, time-consuming, and expensive. Who can you turn to for support if you choose to keep the baby? The baby's father may help, although studies show only 36 percent of teen mothers report daily contact with the father by the time the child is one month old. Sometimes family may offer emotional and financial support.

It is important to think about who you can rely on and develop a number of plans for the future. Some plans will be short term, as in who can help provide child care when you need it. Some will be long term, such as how to finish school or get a good job.

# Adoption Options

Placing your child for adoption also demands enormous sacrifice. If you cannot provide all a child requires but don't want to end the pregnancy, adoption may be the solution. Adoption is arranged through an agency, government, or handled independently. The people who adopt your child go through an extensive process of interviews and background checks to ensure that they are competent and caring. Some of the information you supply to the agency, such as health history or your baby's birth name, is given to the adoptive parents. Confidential, closed adoptions keep the identities of birth parents and adoptive parents secret. Adoption laws vary, depending on the state or province. Finalization of an adoption can take as few as three months or as many as six. In some places, the baby's father or your own parents must give **consent** to the adoption.

Adoptive families can offer stable and loving homes.

# Open Adoption

Another form of adoption is called open adoption, where the birth parent, or parents, and the adopted family know each other and exchange information. Open adoptions are becoming more common because they allow birth parents some contact with the child they have given up. Birth parents give up their legal rights to the child, but enter into an agreement that may include visits and letters. In an open adoption, you may select the adoptive family. In the United States, not all states have laws that protect open adoption agreements. Even with them, adoptive parents have control over contact.

Giving up your baby or deciding to have an abortion are major decisions. It is natural to have second thoughts.

# Abortion

Abortion is a touchy subject that almost everyone has an opinion on. Abortion is a medical termination, or ending, of a pregnancy. It involves expelling or removing the fetus from the uterus. It is a serious surgical procedure that must be done by a doctor in a medical facility.

## Access to Abortion

Abortion is legal in the United States but access varies from state to state. Some states require teens under 18 to have parental permission or parental notification for abortions. Abortion is legal in Canada and does not require parental permission. At the very least, abortion requires pregnant teens to be informed about the procedure and give consent. Statistics show that most abortions (89 percent) are performed within the first 12 weeks of a pregnancy. The longer a pregnant teen waits, the more complicated the procedure. Teens who choose to terminate or end a pregnancy are most likely to do so if they have a parent who supports their decision. The abortion pill is a series of three pills prescribed by a doctor. It can be used to end a pregnancy within seven weeks of your last period.

It is natural for young women who are pregnant, no matter what they decide to do about it, to feel scared, worried, and different from normal. Talking to a parent or another adult you trust, such as a school counselor, can be a big help.

# Chapter 6
## Seeking Help

If you are pregnant, you may be overwhelmed by all the decisions you need to make. Your hormones may have sent your emotions on a roller coaster ride and you may feel alone. Support throughout your pregnancy is important. You need someone you trust to talk to, to answer your questions, and provide guidance.

## Talking About It

It is normal to worry about how others will react to the news that you are pregnant. You may find that some friends are very supportive and others are judgmental. They might even be angry because they believe you made a stupid decision or are throwing your life away. You may find that most will come around after a while. You will need the help of supportive friends to confide in or help affirm your decisions.

"My dad was never around and my mom doesn't have a lot of time. I know I can be a good mom. It will make me more mature. I have some friends who have had kids and I know I can rely on them."
-Talicia, aged 16.

## How to Open Up

It may help to sort through your feelings before you break the news to your family. Sometimes a teacher or school counselor can help you talk things out and direct you to resources in your community. Some schools offer health clinics during school hours. In most cases your discussions will be kept confidential, or private. If you are in danger because of an abusive relationship, or if you threaten to do harm to yourself, teachers are required to inform authorities in order to protect you. If you are concerned about the privacy of your conversation, ask first.

If a friend or girlfriend tells you they are pregnant, don't make them feel bad about themselves. Listen to them. Offer them support. Be willing to go with them to appointments or to hold their hand when telling others they love about their news.

# The Father's Role

It can be sticky telling the baby's father that you are pregnant. Some fathers accept the news without fuss. They may even hope that you choose to keep the baby and raise your child together. Others may react with anger. He might try to blame you or deny that the baby is his. Be prepared for any reaction. If he is older than you, he may try to convince you that it is no big deal, that he will support you and perhaps even marry you. But it is a big deal. It is a life-changing deal for both of you. Having a supportive partner can help you deal with a pregnancy. The baby's father has the right to know you are pregnant and that the baby really is his. If you have the child and keep it, the father has the right to know his child. He also has responsibilities, including the responsibility to help support his child financially.

Many fathers want to be involved in raising their children. Not all will follow through on what they say they are going to do.

# Telling Your Parents

Telling your family that you are pregnant may be one of the hardest conversations of your life. You know your parents and you can guess how they might react. They might feel shame, guilt, or embarrassment. They may be shocked to discover that you are having sex. You probably have some idea how their beliefs and cultural values will influence their reaction.

You probably also know if they will react with anger. If your parents have acted violently in the past, it is important to protect your safety. Have someone with you when you break the news. Your pregnancy was likely a surprise to you, and it will be a surprise to them, too. Give your family time to adjust to the idea. In one study of pregnant teens, 80 percent wrongly predicted how their mothers would react to the news of their pregnancy. Study participants expected negative reactions. In most cases, their mothers were upset, but over time, their attitudes changed to acceptance.

Family and friends might be upset at first, but they may come around after they have had time to accept the facts.

# Step Up to the Plate

When someone you care about tells you they are pregnant, it is easy to judge and shake your finger. Being a good friend, family member, or partner means being supportive and not trying to control them or make decisions for them. Here are some tips that can help you be there for them:

Listen to them and hear them out. Don't cut them off or talk over them. They are telling you because they trust you and you need to know.

It is okay to say you are disappointed or upset. It is not okay to threaten them or force them into a decision that suits you. Try saying things such as, "I'll help you," or "We can work this out."

Help them find resources. Gently suggest they see a doctor and go to the doctor with them if they are afraid. Check out the Web sites listed at the end of this book. Many of them offer help to parents, siblings, and partners.

If you are the father of the baby, do not pressure or threaten your partner into making a decision on the pregnancy that you would prefer. You can tell her what your wishes are, but she is carrying the baby.

Don't say, "Your life is over!" They need help to realize that they can make choices that are good and positive. Don't force them into making decisions they do not feel good about. Encourage them to talk about their hopes.

# Chapter 7
# Coping Toolbox

Sometimes when we are faced with a crisis, we focus on the very worst that could happen. Some people focus on the very best. It is more healthy to consider all possibilities and know how you feel about each. This way you can prepare yourself and work toward the result you want. To do this, ask yourself three questions. You may wish to do this in a journal, so you can look back on your reasons and remind yourself to be strong.

1. What do I hope will happen?

2. What do I think will happen?

3. What am I scared will happen?

For example, consider telling your parents that you are pregnant. You might hope they will understand and support you. If you think they will freak out and be very upset, you need to prepare for this. Remind yourself to stay calm and allow them time to work it through, just as you did. If you are scared that your parents will react violently, be prepared by having someone with you.

# Teen Pregnancy Coping Plan

If you discover you are pregnant, think about what YOU would like to see happen, both for the present and the future. This would be a good task to write down in a journal, if you feel comfortable and safe doing this.

Write down things such as:

How did you feel when you discovered you were pregnant? How do you feel now?

What are your hopes for the future? Do they include this child?

Who can help you: make decisions, get through the day, plan for the future.

Do you want to continue your schooling?

Can you to continue at your school?

Are there special programs for pregnant and parenting teens at schools near you? Who can help direct you to these programs?

If you choose to keep your baby, who can help you find financial support?

If you choose to put your baby up for adoption, where can you go to talk to someone about this?

If you choose to have an abortion, how will you pay for it and where will you go for it?

Write down each issue and problem you have so that you can focus on finding help and solutions.

# Hot Topics
## Q&A

**Q: My girlfriend is pregnant. What should I do?**

A: First, you should be supportive. You may experience a range of emotions and have many questions when you think about this pregnancy. To help work through all this and understand the decisions that need to be made, talk to a trusted adult or counselor. Hotlines and health care centers can help fathers, too.

**Q: Does the pill begin to work the first day I take it? Can I use my sister's birth control pills?**

A: The Pill must be prescribed for you by a doctor to ensure you are taking the one that is right for your body and needs. It must be taken every day, not just when you have sex. It can take up to one month before the birth control pill is effective at preventing pregnancy.

**Q: Can you get pregnant without having intercourse?**

A: Pregnancy can happen any time the penis comes into contact with the vaginal area. It is possible for sperm deposited outside the body to swim into the vagina. Air does not kill sperm immediately. In fact, sperm can live for three to five days in a moist, warm environment.

Q: I want to have an abortion but my parents are religious and would kill me if they find out I was pregnant and had an abortion. I'm scared but I really don't want to have this baby. Should I lie to them?

A: No matter what decision you make about your pregnancy, you will need emotional support from the people around you. They can only provide this if they know what you are going through. An abortion must be done by a qualified professional and may require your parents' permission, depending on the laws where you live. Talk to a counselor who can explain all your options. In the end, though, it is your decision.

Q: I am pregnant and plan to keep my baby, but my parents refuse to support us. What do I do if they kick us out of the house?

A: Many teen moms find themselves alone, without the support of their family or the baby's father. If this worries you, talk to a counselor at school or on the phone. Some government programs offer financial support to mothers. These programs may take time to start, so get information on women's shelters if you need a place to stay immediately.

Q: My boyfriend is nine years older than me and doesn't like to use condoms. I want to trust him, but I'm worried about getting pregnant. What should I do?

A: It is easy to believe that because someone is older they should be wiser. That is not always the case. Can you talk to him honestly about your fears and your desire to prevent pregnancy? If he won't take responsibility, you can take steps to protect yourself by visiting a free clinic or doctor to discuss contraceptive methods. The birth control pill, patch, or shot are effective contraceptive methods, but they do not protect you from STIs.

# Other Resources

There are many Internet sources offering information on teen pregnancy. Be careful though—some Web sites are very one-sided in what they present. Look for organizations that provide information and support. You should not be pressured into making any choices that you are uncertain about. Here are some trustworthy resources. The Web sites will contain useful information no matter which country you live in, but telephone numbers and referral services will be country-specific.

## In the United States

### Planned Parenthood

www.plannedparenthood.org/teen-talk

A section for teens provides information and videos on sexuality, pregnancy, and options, as well as the location of health centers and services.

### Teenshealth.org: sexuality

www.teenshealth.org

This site provides information on your changing body, sexual health, infections, and many other topics.

### Option Line

www.optionline.org

1-800-395-HELP (4357)

This 24-hour-a-day phone, email, or instant messaging help center has Web site information on dating, sex, and pregnancy. Consultants can connect callers with a resource center in their community or nearby.

**Stayteen**
www.stayteen.org
Get informion on dating and relationships, contraception, abstinence planning, and pregnancy.

**American Pregnancy Helpline**
www.thehelpline.org
1-866-942-6466
This is a national free service that offers information on pregnancy, health, and relationships, as well as a 24-hour call-in line.

**The following hotlines can be used in the United States. If you are calling from another part of the world, you may get a referral to another service in your region.**

**Planned Parenthood**
1-800-230-7526

**Option Line**
1-800-395-4357

**National Sexual Assault Hotline**
1-800-656-4673

# In Canada
**Kids Help Phone**
www.kidshelpphone.ca
1-800-668-6868
Support forums for teens will help you see that you are not alone. Anonymous, confidential counseling is also available online. Phone counseling is available only to callers in Canada.

# Glossary

**abstinence** Not having sex

**anemia** A blood condition that makes a person pale and tired

**coerced** To persuade someone to do something using force or threats

**conditional** Something given according to specific terms or requirements

**conscious** To do something deliberately or intentionally

**consent** Agreeing to something or giving permission

**consequences** The result of an action

**developed** Economically or socially advanced

**embryo** An unborn human baby in the first eight weeks from conception

**ethical** Something considered morally correct or according to a person's belief in what is right and wrong

**fallopian tubes** The tubes along which eggs travel from the ovaries to the uterus

**genetic** From genes, or things that are inherited

**hormones** regulatory substances in our bodies that influence sexual function, behavior, and mood

**inhibitions** Something that restrains a person's behavior and impulses

**latex** A type of plastic used for condoms

**nutrients** Substances from foods needed to survive

**placenta** An organ in the uterus that nourishes a baby through the umbilical cord

**poverty** The state of being very poor

**prenatal** Before birth

**puberty** The period during which adolescents reach sexual maturity and are capable of reproducing babies

**sperm** The mature male sex cell

**statutory rape** Sexual intercourse with a minor under the age of consent

**STIs** Sexually transmitted infections, such as herpes or HIV

**terminate** To end something

**ultrasound** A medical tool used to scan and see things inside the human body

**uterus** An organ in females where babies grow; also known as the womb

**virginity pledge** A promise made to not have sex until marriage

# Index